What others are saying about
The Ripple Effect

"This enjoyable, insightful book shows you how to remove the obstacles that can be holding you back from achieving unlimited success."
–Brian Tracy, Author, *No Excuses –*
The Power of Self Discipline

"If you're ready to let go of what's not working in your life and start embracing who you are at your best, this is the book which will empower you to get there. By absorbing and implementing Doug Grady's insight into how making one simple choice can change the course of your life, you can begin living the life you *really* want to live!"
–Ivan Misner, Ph.D., NY Times Bestselling
Author and Founder of BNI®

"The Ripple Effect is a user-friendly guide to the life you've always wanted."
–Dan Lier, Author, *The 10 Minute Coach*

"The Ripple Effect has the power to transform your life. The lively, practical and <u>personal</u> way that Grady shares his life experiences is far more than another checklist of good ideas. Rather, the poignant integration of mind/body/spirit combined with the application of the exercises can actually help you discover your life's purpose."
–Andrew Crowell, Managing Partner, Crowell, Weedon & Co.

"The Ripple Effect is a real-world, highly effective flight plan for breaking performance barriers in your life. If you're looking to reach new heights, read this book, implement its suggestions, and let Doug Grady be your wingman!"
–Lt. Col. Rob "Waldo" Waldman, author of the national bestseller, *Never Fly Solo*

"Doug Grady's advice to make one small improvement at a time is inspired. Too often books ask you to make big, dramatic changes that set you up for failure. But this book is different. You won't be overwhelmed but rather compelled to be your best self. Highly recommended."
–Michael Port, NY Times Bestselling author, *The Big Manifesto*

"Doug Grady writes from his personal experience and that provides a more meaningful message for all the readers. His advice is actionable and will make a difference in your life if you take action too. Life is too short to work with theories, you have to work with proven practical strategies that work; The Ripple Effect is full of those strategies."
–Dominic Carubba, Director, Performance Solutions Center

"The Ripple Effect is the best book ever written to uncover and overcome what is holding you back from reaching your potential. Doug Grady powerfully delivers the elegant, but potent answers to our biggest questions."
–Peter Montoya, Entrepreneur and Author, *The Brand Called You*

"The Ripple Effect is a dynamite book full of compelling stories that will inspire you to reach your true potential. Its powerful ideas will teach you to embrace life's ups and downs and use them as stepping stones for great success. Read this book now to catapult yourself to greatness."
–David Alexander, Co-author of the bestseller, *Networking Like a Pro*

"The Ripple Effect is a personal story that will touch everyone. If you have anything you need to "do" this book will get you started or you are not breathing."
–Michael E. Moore, Rainmaker & Chief Storyteller

Humor, Relevancy and Authentic Vulnerability are the cornerstones of The Ripple Effect. Doug Grady has a paradoxically amazing way of standing outside of his ego and observing his life so that he is humbly reminded that he is a spiritual being having a human experience. He uses his genius and gift of perspective to empower you to stand outside of yourself and witness The Ripple Effect of the choices that you make in your daily life. He then personally examples how to plant TREE's (The Ripple Effect Everyday) that will guarantee a fruitful future for you and everyone that is impacted by your effect.
–Saint Day Adeogba, Founder, YourDay

"I believe a truly successful person produces ripples in the lives of others. That's why I encourage you to read this book and let Doug Grady not only create a ripple in your life but inspire you to create ripples in the lives of others."
–Jon Gordon, Bestselling author,
  The Energy Bus and *The Seed*

"The Ripple Effect shoots straight to the issues that are holding you back in life. After one chapter I changed a behavior that has created so many positive Ripples in my life. Very powerful!"
—Jeff Liesener, CFO (Chief Food Officer), Topline Foods

The Ripple Effect
by Doug Grady

Writing Career Coach Press (a division of Writing Career Coach, 225 West Adrian Street, Blissfield, MI 49228) functions only as book publisher. As such, the ultimate design, content, editorial accuracy, and views expressed or implied in this work are those of the author.

Cover Art by Zakr Studio. www.zakrstudio.com

ISBN 13: 978-0-9833607-9-7
ISBN 10: 0983360790

This book is dedicated to my father.

Introduction

> *So often we want to be*
> *rescued from the storm. We*
> *don't realize it is the storm*
> *that rescues us.*[1]

These words hit me like a thunder bolt. I was in the midst of my own personal storm. It included—among other elements—intense financial pressures, overwhelming feelings of failure, and habits and tendencies that were making things much worse. I felt defeated and completely out of control. I wanted to be rescued.

I remember thinking, *What if this is true? What if this storm really is here to rescue me?*

I have always been fascinated with how we become who we are. What creates breakthroughs in our lives? How do we

---

[1] I heard this in a sermon by Bryan Dunagan. He wasn't sure where it came from, and I have been unable to locate the source.

create a life we are excited about that also makes a powerful, positive difference for others? Why do so many incredibly talented, gifted, and "fortunate" people (insert your favorite Hollywood star's tragedy here) end up ruining their lives? How do others defy the odds and live extraordinary, exemplary lives?

I have studied and taught the pathways to personal potential for over 20 years. I have read hundreds of books and invested thousands of dollars and hours in seminars, training programs, personal coaching, and other "self-help" strategies with the "best" in the business. They have taught me how to think and act successful; how to set goals; how to manage my time; how to communicate more effectively; and how to get more out of myself and others. I was an excellent student and have become a professional speaker and trainer, leading thousands of people all over the country to be more effective in their chosen field of endeavor.

Still somehow, there came a time in my life when I ended up "stuck." I was heavily in debt; my business was losing money; I was physically out of shape; I was drinking excessively; my relationships were suffering; and I had a bad attitude. That was on a good day. Some of my closest friends and advisors were recommending I consider a new career path. I began to ask myself,

"How did I get here?"

I often brooded over the irony of how an intelligent, experienced man in the "success" business could allow himself to be sucked into the quagmire of mediocrity. I wanted desperately to continue to blame it on the economy and bad luck.

Lessons repeat themselves until learned.

My storm carried lessons. Lessons I needed to learn. There were times I hated facing the truth. Some things I already knew, I just didn't want to admit. Others were revealed. My storm shook me; it rocked me; it humbled me.

"When pride comes, then comes disgrace, but with humility comes wisdom."
–Proverbs 11:2

When I got brutally honest with myself, I realized I was the problem. The ripples created from the habitual behaviors I had engaged in and the limiting beliefs I had cultivated had led me to exactly where I was. It was no accident. My mental, emotional, spiritual, physical, and financial state—all of which were suffering—were nothing more than the inevitable result of the choices I had made. I knew something had to change.

I prayed.

I had prayed before, often. I had prayed for guidance, wisdom, and clarity; for the ability to make good decisions. Those may seem like intelligent prayers, but when I prayed them, they were nothing more than various ways of saying, "Help ME get better at getting what I want."

Something was different about this prayer. It came from a different place—a place with no agenda; open to whatever response I received.

Almost immediately I became present to two truths:

1. I had been given much.
2. I was by contrast giving very little.

> "Your talent is God's gift to you. What you do with it is your gift back to God."
>   –Leo Buscaglia

I made one simple choice.

It had been several months since I had exercised consistently. I had been athletic for most of my life but had allowed a hip injury to become an excuse for not exercising. I felt tired, lethargic, flabby, and weak. I made a commitment to exercise a minimum of 30 minutes each day for 30 consecutive days. It was one simple choice.

It was a less than inspired moment. Nonetheless, it was a commitment.

The workouts were initially unpleasant and inconvenient, but I followed through. My daily commitment seemed to attract other positive choices. I found myself eating healthier and getting up earlier. Other ripples followed: reading something positive each day, becoming more active in my church, practicing my music, writing. I committed to making a minimum of 20 prospecting calls each business day. I attended three to six networking meetings each week. I let go of some bad habits. Some of those changes simply "happened" without much thought, planning, or work on my part. Others (the calls for example) took more conscious effort.

> "Sow a thought and you reap an action; sow an act and you reap a habit; sow a habit and you reap a character; sow a character and you reap a destiny."
> –Ralph Waldo Emerson

I began to think more clearly; my energy increased; my communication became more effective; people began to respond differently to me. I met (and now hang out with) some extraordinary people I never would have met otherwise. Oh, and my business started moving in the right direction. One choice led to other choices and to a series of positive outcomes. The ripples changed the course of my life.

> "After a storm comes a calm."
> –Matthew Henry

That storm has passed. As a direct result, I have a significantly healthier lifestyle, a stronger sense of purpose, and better relationships with the important people in my life. In its wake it left a positive, lasting impact on every aspect of my life. The storm has passed, the ripples continue.

Within this book there are stories of storms, lessons, and the ripples that followed. They range from childhood incidents to incidents

in the very recent past. You may find
yourself somewhere in the midst of them.

This is the ripple effect.

How to get the most out of this book

> "Your life will never make
> sense until you look in the rear
> view mirror."
>
> –Steve Jobs

Consider your life as a series of ripples. The experiences in your life and your response to them have led you to where you are now. It is not an accident.

This book explores three basic questions.

1. **How did you get here?** As you read, reflect on the choices you have made and how they have affected your life.
2. **Where are you going?** Think about the life you really want. Allow yourself to become inspired.
3. **How will you get there?** Choose. One simple choice can change the course of your life.

Take your time. Read each segment thoughtfully and deliberately. Keep a journal nearby to secure your thoughts. Share with others what is happening in your life.

Cliff Diving: Your Higher Purpose

When I was eight years old, our family was vacationing in Chattanooga, TN at Cloudland State Park near Lookout Mountain. My older brother decided to climb up the side of a rocky cliff and sibling rivalry left me no choice but to chase after him. We were up about 20 feet or so when my father told us to come down. I won that race by losing my footing and falling head first onto the rocks below. I suffered a concussion, a couple of broken ribs, and some heavy bruises but was discharged from the emergency room the same day.

I was rushed back to the hospital a couple of days later after I told my mother I felt strange. A visiting specialist at the hospital determined I had a collapsed lung, a ruptured spleen, and I was bleeding internally. The doctors performed an emergency splenectomy, and I spent nine days in the hospital recovering. My parents were later informed of just how close a call that was. If not for the accurate diagnosis from the visiting doctor (who just happened to be there), it is likely I would have died.

> "Definiteness of purpose is the starting point of all achievement."
> –W. Clement Stone

I never really thought much about some of the comments my mother made from time to time throughout my youth and into my adulthood. She had told me she knew God had a plan for me because I had come so close to death but was still here. I think about those words now. What if she was right? What if God has a plan for me? What if God has a plan for you? People die every day. Why are we still here?

> "Everything in the universe has a purpose. Indeed, the invisible intelligence that flows through everything in a purposeful fashion is also flowing through you."
> –Wayne Dyer

What if you are here for a purpose; a higher purpose; one far beyond your personal goals, aspirations, and ambitions? What if you absolutely knew this is to be true? What would happen if you tuned into this purpose fully?

For many people, this is a big, often overwhelming concept. For others, it can seem irrelevant. Purpose can lie buried in the muck and the mire of setback and disappointment. It can get lost in the clouds of superficial success and prosperity. Here are some less daunting questions which may help you reconnect with your purpose.

- When do you feel most alive? "Rowing"
  - creating designs
  - helping people get on track w/ their money/retirement plan.
- Who are you at your best?
  - working out daily / rowing
  - playing piano
  - eating/drinking healthy
  - w/ family & friends
  - doing what makes me feel most alive.

- What qualities do you want to develop?

[handwritten] - public speaking
- patience, tolerance
- financial knowledge

- What do you do naturally that affects others in a positive way?

[handwritten] - my spiritual insights
- caring for others

- What moves you to the core?

[handwritten] Injustice to others

- What subjects do you enjoy learning about and studying?

[handwritten] Spiritual study

- What would you do with your life if money were not a factor?

[handwritten] ❀ Coach / F.A.
❀ designer

- What causes are you drawn to? Why?

Helping PEOPLE get their $ on track.

- Who do you most admire? Why?

working w/ young people

- How do you want the world to be different because of you?

- feminizing the FEMINIZING financial Services. Educating people to get started early

- What legacy do you want to leave behind? *-*

That I helped people take care of Biz

- If you could start again, what would you do differently?

START EARLIER in my Retirement Plan

"It's never too late to be what you might have been."
–George Eliot

Here are several practices I consistently engage in to connect/reconnect with my higher purpose:

- Prayer/meditation
- Reading the Bible
- Attending church
- Exercising
- *The Self-confidence Formula*, from *Think and Grow Rich*
- Yoga
- Journal writing
- Listening to music, playing my banjo, and singing
- Experiencing nature
- Studying and learning from people who are living a higher purpose
- Volunteering for causes I believe in

For some people, it takes a near death experience to get connected to their purpose. Many others die never having come close. Here's to you living your higher purpose.

Do it Anyway

Emotions are powerful. They can infuse passion, purpose, and power into our daily activities or they can be the precursor to a sense of futility and failure, tempting us to give up. As you strive to keep your daily commitments, you may experience an emotional roller coaster. The ride won't always be pleasant. Here are some thoughts on staying on track whether you feel like it or not.

> "Do it anyway."
> –Rev. Donald E. Grady, Sr.
> (My Dad)

How I hated those words! They usually came after I told my father I didn't want to do something like clean my room, eat my vegetables, mow the lawn, clean the dishes, chop wood, and other such tasks. I would say something like "I hate broccoli" or "I don't want to clean my room" or "I don't feel like mowing the lawn" or "I'm tired." His response, "Do it anyway." How many times have you not done something you knew you should have done simply because you didn't feel like it?

Feelings can be misleading. Do you know the hardest aspect of exercise for most people? It's not the physical act of exercise. It's getting to the gym. For most people, once they get to the gym it is significantly easier to work out. The pre-workout feelings often instill a sense that the task will be far more unpleasant, difficult, or tedious than it actually is. I don't always feel like going to the gym, but I generally feel great when I leave after a workout.

You may not feel like sticking with your commitments. You may not feel like you are making progress. You may not feel like doing the things you know you need to do. You may have to take your feelings out of it. You may at times feel irritable, frustrated, agitated, overwhelmed, exasperated, confused, and befuddled. Do it anyway. Honoring your word feels good, and knowing you are making progress despite your "feelings" feels good. Hitting one of your major goals feels FANTASTIC.

Here are some of the "feelings" you may experience:

- It doesn't feel like I am making progress. This stops many people. If you don't feel like you are making progress, why bother? The next logical outcome is to quit. Remember, you will not always feel like you are making progress. Do it anyway.
- It feels like today might be a good day to take the day off. "I've been working so hard, I think I've done enough today, this week, this month…" Do it anyway.
- I feel too tired to (exercise, write, make prospecting calls…). Thanks for sharing—do it anyway.
- Yesterday was such a (great, horrid, tedious, extraordinary, awful, fill in the blank) day that I deserve a day off. Yes, Princess, of course you do. Do it anyway.

I now hear and listen to those words "Do it anyway" when I don't feel like doing something like:

- Writing
- Exercising
- Making prospecting calls
- Studying
- Doing paperwork
- Cleaning (well- this one I generally pay someone to do)

It never ceases to amaze me how many extraordinary things happen when I act in the face of not feeling like it. Some of my most effective days booking meetings over the phone have been when I called purely because I said I would. Several of my best written articles and a couple of physical breakthroughs in the gym came on days I did not feel like it but did it anyway.

Success tends to take disciplined, consistent action over long periods of time. Commitment has little to do with feeling. Commitment means you do it anyway— whether you feel like it or not; whether it is *like RAising kids —*

easy or not; whether it is pleasant or not;
whether you are too busy or not; whether
you are tired or not; whether it is convenient
or not. When you consistently do what you
say you are going to do, you develop
confidence, inner strength, momentum, and
ultimately character.

*Regardless of how
I feel, I got up everyday
to take care of them.*

Wrestling with Self-esteem

I was a shy, introverted, insecure kid. My parents encouraged academics, music, and intellectual pursuits. That included "gifted" classes, choir, band, and piano lessons—all worthwhile, but they did little to change my geek status. I wanted to be popular, confident, and comfortable in social settings.

In eighth grade, I joined the wrestling team. One of the most popular kids in school, Keith Hamrick, was a wrestler and also my friend. I did my best to learn from his confidence. I excelled in wrestling and that helped tremendously. The success in wrestling combined with my friendship with Keith proved to be the recipe for confidence in my youth.

> "Our greatest victories are won not over circumstances or other people but over ourselves."
>
> –Doug Grady

I remember one of my defining moments in high school. The football team was brought into the wrestling room to cross-train. One of the football players, an unpleasant kid, had a particular disliking for me, partly because his girlfriend had a particular liking for me. I was actually a little scared of him. He had at least 30 lbs. on me, was significantly stronger than I was, and was one mean son of a gun. But by that time, I was a very good wrestler. As fate would have it, I was positioned against him in a wrestle-off. I mopped the mat with that boy—threw him around like a rag doll. He never bothered me again. It went a long way to fueling my inner strength and positive self-esteem.

Think of a struggle you faced in your youth.

- What was it?

Being bullied by big black girls / growing up w/ girl

- How did you learn from it?

Who I didnt want to be.

- How did you grow?

  STronger, inner strength

- Who helped you along the way?

  my aunt, grandmother

Perhaps you are currently "wrestling" something. You may be facing off with an addiction, a failed relationship, a financial crisis, or the loss of a loved one. These same four questions can help you to fight the good fight.

- What is it? Clarify exactly what you are facing. What are the emotions you are wrestling with? Are you present to fear? Frustration? Grief? Loss? Be specific and be brutally honest.

  Financial insecurity FEAR all of the above

- How can you learn from this?

get my shit in order

- How can you grow?

stay committed to my chord to get in the industry & develop my strengths, purpose, passion

- Who can help you through it?

Julie / Nik
Matt / Michael

Our greatest victories are won not over circumstances or other people but over ourselves. The battles we face are here to cleanse us, to shape and mold us, to help us grow. <u>They are preparing us for what's next. Keep fighting the good fight, and never give up.</u>

Fail Your Way to Success

David was a beast of a boy. We attended the same school in 8th grade, my first year as a wrestler. (I think David began wrestling at age 2 or 3.) He was strong and mean and took great pleasure in throwing me all over the mat in practice. Two years later as a sophomore in a different high school, I found myself up against him in the finals of a tournament. To most people's surprise, including my own, I was winning comfortably in the 3rd and final round. With less than 15 seconds left in the match, however, David stuck me with a double under-hook, flipped me to my back, and pinned me. It was devastating.

> "The events we bring upon ourselves, no matter how unpleasant, are necessary in order to learn what we need to learn; whatever steps we take, they're necessary to reach the places we've chosen to go."
> –Richard Bach

[handwritten: SOUL = Goal Achievement — Accountability]

The dictionary defines failure as "The condition or fact of not achieving the desired end or ends." That loss certainly qualified. If you are challenged by a recent (or not so recent) failure, consider taking yourself through this process and recording your reflections in your journal:

1. **Distinguish a failure.**

   [handwritten: Not planning for my RETIREMENT.]

2. **Evaluate your natural tendencies.**

   - What do you do when you fail?

     [handwritten: Eat popcorn, drink wine, do a jegsaw puzzle, walk the beach]

   - Where do you go mentally and emotionally?

     [handwritten: feel like a loser]

- What do you make it mean about you, the result, and the world you live in? *what a fraud I am - trying to help others when I haven't done it myself.*

- What do you say to yourself? *Better make sure kids commit to help me if I don't figure it out in next 10 yrs*

- How does it tend to change the course of your life? *makes it hard to get up*

3. **Look for the lessons.** Perhaps you've heard the phrase "lessons repeat themselves until learned." Take the stance that there is a lesson here and you can learn it. Be brutally honest.

- Have you found yourself in a similar dilemma in the past?

- What are the common
  denominators that contributed to
  you ending up here?

- Are there tendencies, habits, or
  areas of neglect which led you
  here?

Ignorance

4. **Pull yourself out of the picture.**
   Step back and see yourself in a
   movie. You are now watching the
   hero (you) struggle with a seemingly
   insurmountable challenge.

   - What strengths, people,
     strategies, and other resources
     can our hero call on?

- What do you need?

- Who can you ask for help?

- Create a soundtrack for your road toward victory. What songs did you choose?

5. **Develop an "attitude of gratitude."** Be thankful for the experience. Believe it is here to help and serve you. Ask yourself:

- What am I doing right?
  getting up everyday

- What's great about this?

- What's funny about this that I haven't noticed yet?

  I'm trying to teach people to do what I havent!!

- What can I learn from this?

  It's given me my passion

- What am I grateful for?

  My kids, family, good friends

6. **Apply the lessons.** Ask for help. Grow.

  LEAF

- Who can I count on?

  Julie / Nik

- Who has gone through a similar situation? How can I learn from his or her experience?

- Who can I ask for help?

- How can I grow?

- How can I be a positive impact for others because of this?

  Tell my story

- What am I committed to?

  making sure my kids dont go through what I did. Or anyone else I meet.

I wish I could tell you I wrestled David again and avenged my loss. Or that I became the greatest wrestler ever. The fact is: I never even saw him again. What I did do was get help. I got coached. I got stronger. I got better. I was never pinned again and was eventually ranked 3rd in my weight class in the state of Alabama.

More than anything else in my youth, wrestling instilled in me a sense of confidence, discipline, mental toughness, leadership, and perseverance. There is no doubt in my mind I became a better wrestler and a better person because of that loss. To this day whenever I get "pinned," that match reminds me to get up, dust myself off, learn, grow, and get back in the ring.

> "I never failed once, it just happened to be a 2000 step process."
> –Thomas Edison

Now get out there and fail! It is your pathway to greatness.

The First Step

> "There never was a winner
> who was not first a beginner."
> –Dr. Denis Waitley

My friend Eddie V has been singing and playing guitar and harmonica for over a decade now. He is one of my favorite people to watch perform or do a little "pickin and grinnin" with. His passion for music, however, was almost never realized. Eddie became interested in playing the guitar in his late 20s. He figured conservatively it would take at least 5 to 6 years to become decent at it and because of that he almost didn't take the first step. It was his mother who encouraged him. She said, "Eddie, Lord willing, you'll be here five or six years from now anyway; you might as well learn guitar." Eddie V is still here and plans to continue to perform for many years to come.

> "The journey of a thousand miles begins with a single step."
> –Lao Tzu

The Ripple Effect

Are you finding it difficult to take that first step toward a new venture, an unrealized passion, an exercise program, or the elimination of a bad habit? What's holding you back? What stops you from taking the first step? Here are a few obstacles that have affected me at one time or another:

- Being overwhelmed. Read the Lao Tzu quote again and focus on the "thousand miles." How does that make you feel? Now focus on the "single step." Do you notice a difference? You don't have to have it all figured out. Simply take the first step.

  growing old broke.

- Fear of _____. Fill in the blank. What is it for you? Failure? Looking bad? Loss? It may not work out? Isolate your fear(s). Instead of resisting them, try embracing them. In my mind, it goes something like this, "I may fail; I may look bad; I may lose; it may not work out. So what? I'm going to go for it!" Take the first step.

- Comparing myself to others. Hey, when I listen to Earl Scruggs play the banjo, I have a choice. I can be depressed or inspired. Which do you think is more empowering? Take the first step.

- Staying in my comfort zone. This is simply another way of saying you're just too lazy to do anything about your aspirations. Reaching your potential in any endeavor will take hard work. Put down the remote, log out of Facebook, get off the couch, and take the first step.

The Ripple Effect

There is tremendous power in taking that first step. Without it, you will never fully realize your potential in the area of your life you are contemplating right now. Yes, that one. With it, your journey has begun. This is where all great journeys begin. Take the first step.

fearing the first
step & knowing what
the first step is

Progress

In July of 2011, I started doing yoga an average of twice a week. My ninth class seemed particularly difficult—maybe even tougher than my first session. It bothered me. I began asking myself all sorts of not so empowering questions: "Why is this so hard? When does this get easier? Why is this taking so long?" Various versions of:

> "How come I haven't made more progress!?!?"
> –One of the Voices in my Head

When it comes to learning a new skill, a new discipline, taking on a new initiative, or letting go of a bad habit, progress can be elusive. I have come to three conclusions about progress. While they may seem obvious, frustration can often cloud our perspective.

"Be not afraid of growing slowly, be afraid only of standing still."
                –Chinese Proverb

1. **Progress doesn't always look or feel like progress.** Realizing our personal definition of progress often takes longer than we expect. Progress sometimes means letting go of our preconceived notions of how far we should have come by now. To get where you want to go, understand where you are without delusion or judgment. Consider expanding your definition of progress. Look for victories, no matter how seemingly small, and acknowledge yourself for even slight movements forward.

2. **Progress is not always steady.** You may fall before you rise. You may fail often to succeed only once. You may take two steps backward to take one step forward. Learn from each setback. Listen to coaches and mentors who have mastery in the area in which you are growing. Raise your awareness. Gain distinctions. Ask yourself, "What did I do right? What could I have done differently? Apply the lessons.

3. **Progress is often made simply by consistently showing up.** You never know when and where significant progress will occur. Keep showing up; continue to practice; train consistently. This exponentially increases the opportunity for progress compared to dabbling in disciplines once in awhile. Relax. Be patient. Keep showing up. A breakthrough is right around the corner.

"If I had permitted my failures, or what seemed to me at the time a lack of success, to discourage me I cannot see any way in which I would ever have made progress."

–Calvin Coolidge

The Breakthrough

> *break•through* (noun):
> 1. A sudden, dramatic, and important discovery or development.
> 2. A significant and dramatic overcoming of a perceived obstacle, allowing the completion of a process.
> –Dictionary.com

And finally it happens. It is unmistakable. You hit a new high, the next level, your stretch goal. You break through.

I have been working out with my personal trainer, Day Adeogba, for over a year now. He has the uncanny ability through a variety of methods to radically accelerate my fitness progress. That is one of the major benefits of having a coach or mentor in the important areas of your life. A recent workout with Day proved to be a breakthrough session. It was undeniable. I was stronger, more energized, and needed less recovery time between sets. I reached a level on two exercises that was significantly higher than any previous measurement. It felt incredible.

> "Today is the day."
> –Mel Fisher, the world's
> greatest treasure hunter

1. **Distinguish a personal breakthrough**. Maybe you overcame a fear, broke a bad habit, mastered a new skill, received a promotion, or exceeded a business goal. It can be mental, physical, emotional, or otherwise. Any breakthrough will do. Don't read any further until you have one specific breakthrough in mind.

STARTING back to gym
Breaking 10K month mark

2. **How is your experience of a breakthrough different than that of "failure"?**

feeling of well being -

"If you are ever capable of
something, you were always
capable of it."

–Doug Grady

3. **How did this breakthrough
   happen?** Realize it was in you all
   along. If you are ever capable of
   something, you were always capable
   of it. Take the position it was not an
   accident. You were a cause in the
   matter. You made it happen. What
   else might you be capable of? List all
   the elements which contributed to
   your breakthrough. Visualize the
   path that brought you here.
   Acknowledge all your hard work, the
   distinctions you gained along the
   way, the people who helped you.

   • What challenges did you
     overcome?

   getting back to gym

The voice said:

I don't have the time to do what I love because I have to make $.

- Who helped you?

  LEFT

- What did you learn?

  to REACH out & Ask for help

- What made this moment possible?

  Timing

- How does it feel?

  good

  Empowered

- How did your mental and emotional make up factor in?

  I just gave up. I let the inner voice take over

- Listen to the voice in your head. What is it saying?

  Dont forget to pay attention to your:
  * creativity   * piano
  * Running   *
  * working out.

- Close your eyes. What do you see? It is critical that you associate with the feelings and sensations you receive when you break through. Notice them. Feel them. Experience them. Appreciate them. Share them with a trusted friend.

- Recognize and give credit to anything and everything involved in this outcome.

4. **Reward yourself.** What gets rewarded gets repeated. Even if some time has passed, it is not too late to reward yourself.

5. *Now what?*

"The best time to make a sale
is right after you made a sale."
–Brian Tracy

The same could be said of a breakthrough.
The energy of a breakthrough attracts other
breakthroughs. A breakthrough in one area
of your life is often the catalyst for
significant, unexpected progress in other
areas. Get, be, and stay ready. Your next
breakthrough awaits.

Unseen Forces: How to Quit Smoking and Run a Marathon

"Until one is committed, there is hesitancy, the chance to draw back, always ineffectiveness. Concerning all acts of initiative (and creation), there is one elementary truth the ignorance of which kills countless ideas and splendid plans: that the moment one definitely commits oneself, then providence moves too. All sorts of things occur to help one that would never otherwise have occurred. A whole stream of events issues from the decision, raising in one's favor all manner of unforeseen incidents and meetings and material assistance, which no man could have dreamed would have come his way. Whatever you can do or dream you can, begin it.

Boldness has genius, power
and magic in it. Begin it now".
—J. W. von Goethe

The year was 2003. I was living in
California building High Achievers Network
when I received an email from a fraternity
brother. He challenged me to fill out the
lottery application for the New York City
marathon, adding that it was the second
most difficult marathon to get into without
qualifying. He reasoned that if I got in
through the lottery system, it was meant to
be. Well, I tend to believe that sort of thing,
so I thought, *What the heck?* I sent in my
application and pretty much forgot about it.

Fast forward three months: High Achievers
Network was hosting a Jack Canfield
seminar. He was speaking on his book **The
Power of Focus**. That book contains a
section on eliminating bad habits, and I
decided to take on quitting smoking. (At that
time I was smoking roughly a pack and a
half a day.) My master plan: start on Sunday
at 20 cigarettes per day and gradually wean
myself down to being smoke free within a

week. Wednesday of that week I received an email. "Congratulations, you're in the New York City marathon!" I thought, *Wow, it looks like I picked the right week to quit smoking.*

I had never considered myself much of a runner. I did a couple of 10Ks in my 20s but it had been years since I had run more than three miles in one stretch. My track record with smoking was much more consistent and committed—an average of a pack a day for the better part of 16 years.

Saturday was to be the day I smoked my last cigarette. I smoked it before 9am. By 9:01am I wanted another one. Instead of smoking, I went to Sports Authority and bought a $160 pair of running shoes. I vowed to destroy the shoes if I ever smoked another cigarette. Less than four months later, I ran (and completed) the New York City Marathon. And yes, I am still a non-smoker.

Without that unexpected email, it is quite possible I would have caved in to my old bad habit. When you take on something big in your life, be ready, be aware, and look for the "unseen forces" that come to your aid.

The High Achievers Goal Setting Formula

In December of 2010, I registered for a run called the Tough Mudder, billed as "Probably the Toughest One Day Run on the Planet." Modeled after British Special Forces Training, it features conquering over 12 miles of grueling terrain in the North Georgia Mountains with 18 obstacles, and a lot of mud. When I shared my plan with a friend, he said, "I'm not ready for that!" I said, "I'm not ready for it either—that's why I registered!"

What's the hardest aspect of completing a marathon, a triathlon, or a Tough Mudder? If you have ever completed one, you already know. In most cases, it is not the "run" itself. It is (wait for it…) the training; the daily discipline of consistent, purposeful exercise. What's the hardest aspect of hitting your goals? It is the daily discipline of consistent, purposeful effort.

After registering for the Tough Mudder, something happened to my workouts almost immediately. They became more intense, more focused, and more purposeful. They also became more fun! Both consciously and unconsciously I began to "step it up." I began to look forward to my workouts. They became less of a "to-do" and more of a "get to." An interesting thing happens when you step up your training. Your life tends to step up as well. On March 12, 2011, I completed my first Tough Mudder.

What's your level of certainty when you set goals? How do you feel when you are striving for something out of your current reach? What's the difference in registering for the Tough Mudder and a typical "goal-setting" experience? Consider the following:

- I registered: I filled out an online application and sent it in with a $150 non-refundable payment. That got it out of my head and into reality.
- I knew exactly when and where it would take place.
- It was on my calendar.
- I let others know I was doing it.

- I started training (taking action) the
  same day.

Champion athletes visualize winning in
advance. Self-help books tell us to write our
own eulogy. The late great comedian
George Burns actually booked himself to
play the London Palladium as a 100th
Birthday celebration. Perhaps you've had
the experience of being extraordinarily
effective the week before a vacation. These
are ways of creating our future in advance.
Our future affects our present.

Consider today creating an inspiring,
definite future for yourself—one that gives
you meaning, purpose, and passion right
now.

One Tough Mudder

On Saturday, March 12, 2011, I completed my first Tough Mudder in Cedartown, GA. Modeled after British Special Forces training, it was a grueling course with 18 obstacles in the North Georgia mountains. When I first wrote about the Tough Mudder, I was convinced that the hardest part about completing the run would be the training. I was wrong. My first marathon was tough (small "t"). This run was TOUGH—way tougher than my training. I guess there's a reason they don't call it the somewhat difficult mudder. I can only imagine how tough it would have been if I had not trained.

My 18-week regimen prior to the Mudder included strength, core, speed, endurance, and flexibility training. It did not include mud pits, ice cold lakes, rocks in my shoes, crawling under barbed wire, or electroshock therapy. (I'm not kidding; that was one of the obstacles!) The 14+ miles (falsely advertised as 12 miles) with the crawling, slipping, falling, climbing, and swimming took me over three-and-a-half hours to complete. It wasn't pretty; it wasn't pleasant; but I am thrilled I did it.

Several people, particularly those who saw me hobbling around on Sunday, asked me why I did it. Here's why: when I am at my best as a man, I am consistently challenging myself with intense physical exercise. Training for and completing the Tough Mudder has created breakthroughs in my life mentally, physically, emotionally, professionally, and spiritually. This is the essence of the ripple effect: one simple choice can change the course of your life.

No matter where you are, there is always another level. Training gets you there. Training for something tough and completing it gets you there quicker. Life can be tough. Train tough. Get tough. Complete tough. Repeat.

The Ripple Effect

Another Tough Mudder

"I'll do it if you do it."

Those were my words to my friend Jason. As I said, my first Tough Mudder was March 12, 2011 in Cedartown, GA. I was confident I would **not** be running my second on September 18th in Squaw Valley, CA. I was wrong. Three weeks after our initial conversation, Jason posted on Facebook that he was doing the Tough Mudder NorCal. I was in.

Preparation for my second Mudder included yoga, nutrition adjustments, strength training, cardio, stretching, and two grueling sessions per week with my good friend and trainer, Day Adeogba. Jason's training consisted of the occasional 12 ounce curls and runs to the fridge. By his own admission, he was not in great shape. At least four close friends tried to talk him out of it for fear of his safety. He said there were three different times he almost quit. But on September 18, 2011, after 5 hours and 52 minutes, Jason was a Tough Mudder.

I was impressed. I honestly wasn't sure he would finish. I knew he could, I just wasn't sure he would. It made me ponder that people are capable of much more than they give themselves credit for, or at least more than they are experiencing.

What else are you capable of?

But it bothered me. Why didn't my friend train for the Tough Mudder? I know him pretty well, and I think he is wired much the same as I am. I thought for sure once he registered it would shift his lifestyle almost automatically to prepare. That is the main component of the High Achievers Goal setting formula. And then it hit me:

He never registered. He never *really* threw his hat in the ring.

Jason didn't actually sign up for the Tough Mudder until the day the event took place. Yes, we had talked about it. Yes, we said we were doing it. He probably had it on his calendar. He even posted it on Facebook. But he hadn't really committed, at least not officially. How would his experience have been different if he had registered earlier? I can only speculate.

Here are some of my favorite JG quotes:

> "If I survive this, I am going to get in shape."
> "My legs felt like tree trunks."
> "I thought aliens were coming out of my calves on mile six."
> "I could feel my heartbeat in my groin."
> "The water was so cold I haven't seen my testicles since Sunday."
>
> –Jason Gray

Looking back, if he could do it all over again, I'm guessing Jason would have prepared more extensively. We may never know. When asked if he would ever do it again, his response was, "Hell no!" The bottom line: neither one of us would have done it if it had not been for the other person. The end result was an extraordinary day on a beautiful mountain with one of my best friends. I can confidently speak for both us that we are glad we did it.

Find something cool or challenging to do. Find someone cool to do it with. Lead with "I'll do it if you do it."

How to Choose a Trainer, Coach, or Mentor

> "You will be the same person
> you are today in five years
> from now except for the people
> you meet and the books you
> read."
> –Charlie "Tremendous" Jones

Let me tell you about a friend of mine. His name is Day Adeogba. I first met Day one week into my commitment to exercise after having led a sedentary lifestyle for several months. Day was leading a Saturday morning "boot camp" that a friend had invited me to. The session was extremely challenging to say the least. Some of the exercises I was physically incapable of, others I struggled through. I barely made it through the hour without getting sick or passing out. Since that time, I have worked out with Day an average of once a week for almost two years. I'm absolutely certain I have made progress with him that I would not have made on my own.

Here's why:

1. He has knowledge I do not have.

2. He has a level of health and fitness I do not have. This provides inspiration and an example of what is possible.

3. He leads exercises I don't do on my own (many of which I never would have thought of).

4. His expectations of me are often higher than those I set for myself.

5. He has a scoring system which monitors and encourages progress.

6. His workouts are so challenging that I tend to push myself harder when I'm exercising on my own.

7. No matter how much progress I make, he always throws something in that is beyond my current capabilities.

The above criteria may be helpful for you when choosing a trainer, a mentor, or a coach. Our natural tendency quite often is to push ourselves only to a certain point. With good people around us, we can exponentially expand our personal and professional growth and create breakthrough results.

All the Green Lights and a Couple of Blue Ones

Have you ever had one of those days when you hit all the green lights? When progress seemed effortless? When you were simply unstoppable? Sometimes it helps to slow down.

I live in an area of Atlanta called Buckhead near Peachtree Rd, one of the busiest streets in Atlanta. There are exactly 17 traffic lights on the three-and-a-half mile stretch between my home and my destination. I was running late for a meeting one morning, heading north on Peachtree. Never in my 10+ years in Atlanta had I ever had the experience of hitting all the green lights on that road, until that day. It was like the parting of the Red Sea—every light was green! I couldn't believe my good fortune as I raced toward my destination unencumbered by those irritating red lights. According to my calculations, I might make it to my meeting with a minute to spare! At the height of my excitement, approaching green light #11, I noticed several additional lights of the color blue flashing in my rear view mirror. The nice officer gave me a yellow piece of paper which read "57 in a 35 mile an hour zone."

That got me thinking. What if the obstacles along the way to our goals were actually there to help us? Is there such thing as getting to your goals too quickly? What if the pain of delay is actually saving you from a far greater pain?

There were three "P's" I lacked on the way to my goal:

1. Preparation: Leaving just seven minutes earlier would have provided me with plenty of time to make it to my meeting.
2. Presence: I was not present to my speed or to the fact that Peachtree Road tends to have a very high number of patrol cars.
3. Patience: My impatience led me to drive well over the legal limit and to a costly speeding ticket. Not to mention that I was much later to my

meeting than I would have been if I had simply slowed down.

Lack of one of those "P's" can be a stumbling block on the way to your goals. Lack of all three can be a recipe for disaster. They all feed into one another. We tend to have an unconscious need to compensate for a lack of preparation with a rushed, often reckless acceleration.

Let my lesson be a reminder for you on the way to your goals:

- Prepare. Anticipate obstacles in advance. Remember Murphy's Law (anything that can go wrong will).
- Be present. Pay attention to your progress, your environment, and the law.
- Be patient. Success may take longer than you planned. When you learn the lessons from the obstacles along the way, you arrive at your goals at just the right time. Most importantly, you develop the characteristics and

qualities necessary to sustain success.

Facing Frustration

> "Frustration, although quite painful at times, is a very positive and essential part of success."
>
> –Bo Bennett

I was having a particularly frustrating day wrestling; no, it was more like I was obsessing over two very uncomfortable circumstances in my life. One was personal, the other a major challenge with my business. I felt completely overwhelmed and out of control in both areas and found myself dwelling on my problems for the better part of the business day. After five or six hours of very low productivity and dismal solitude, I began to look at myself. I was clearly playing the victim. Here's the funny thing. I made a conscious decision to continue to wallow for the rest of the day. I even started a text to a trusted friend. It read:

"I have decided to be a victim today. I will let what happened to me determine how I feel. If something good happens later, maybe I will feel good; if not, I will not.

Feel free to contribute something positive so I can feel better."

I started laughing as I wrote. It just sounded so absurd. I almost couldn't believe I wrote it without trying to be funny. The simple act of consciously choosing to continue my pity party and stating it to a trusted friend completely shifted the experience for me. I felt more power, had a better attitude, and created a complete state change. I didn't even send the text.

> "What you resist persists."
> –Carl Jung

Here's what I think happened:

1. I allowed myself some slack. I had already killed most of the day, so I figured why not finish it off, but at least do it *consciously*.
2. I stated my frustration to someone I trusted.
3. I was able to laugh at myself.

"If we allow our feelings to
pass through us, accept them,
and release them, we shall
know what to do next."
                    –Melody Beattie

The next time you find yourself putting up
with, avoiding, or resisting a feeling of
frustration, try embracing it for a specified,
limited period of time. Reach out to
someone who cares about you. And try not
to take yourself too seriously.

Inspiration

Not too long ago, I was at a seminar. The speaker, leadership guru John Maxwell, had a simple yet profound point: Take personal responsibility for your own happiness. He told a beautiful story of how his wife had come to the realization that external factors could never make her truly happy. She could not count on her family, her work, or her environment to make her happy. But if she was personally responsible for her own happiness, those factors had the ability to enhance her happiness significantly. Her whole life changed when she chose to take personal responsibility for her own happiness.

> "Take personal responsibility
> for your own happiness."
> –Margaret Maxwell

Simple? Yes. Inspiring? Absolutely! Powerful? Oh yeah! Profound? So profound! "Wow, this can change my life forever! All I need to do is take personal responsibility for my own happiness, personal responsibility for my own happiness, personal responsibility for my own happiness, personal responsibility for my own happiness," I kept saying to myself in my best Rainman impression. I was truly inspired! I left the seminar absolutely certain that that principle was the key to my happiness and would change the course of my life. And it did—for about an hour—until someone cut me off in traffic on the way home.

Why is it that the simple, profound, inspiring moments that we truly believe will change our lives forever sometimes end up forgotten? How do we make the flashes of enlightenment last? Is the road to hell really paved with good intentions?

> "Life moves pretty fast. If you don't stop and look around once in a while, you could miss it."
> —Ferris Bueller

Inspiration can be fleeting. Here are some thoughts on living an inspired life:

- Allow yourself to be inspired. Give yourself permission to "stop and smell the roses." In the stresses and struggles of everyday life, it is easy to filter out the many potentially inspiring moments which come and pass. A song on the radio, a conversation with a friend, a seemingly random article in a waiting room magazine—these are all experiences which have changed the course of my life.

- Pay attention to what inspires you. How and when do you tend to be inspired? Ask yourself, "Who inspires me? When have I been inspired in the past? What am I most inspired about right now? What could I allow myself to be inspired about? When do I feel most inspired?"

- Have multiple sources you can draw from for inspiration. My friend Steve Cesari calls this an "inspirational arsenal."

- Do something. Inspiration without action is like being all dressed up with nowhere to go. That little voice is telling you something. What is it? Create a clear future for yourself fueled by your inspiration. Do something immediately to move toward that future. Take the first step.

Steve Cesari's Inspirational Arsenal

1. Quotes
2. Inspirational Scrapbook
3. Movies
4. Biographies
5. The Bible

6. Exercise
7. Prayer
8. PMN (Positive Mental Nutrition and self-talk)
9. Inspiring People
10. Music
11. 12. 13… (What would you add to this list?)

While these suggestions may help, you will not always be inspired. Many people romanticize achievement and growth into a "Rocky-esque" montage of inspired moments. The fact is, we may feel quite uninspired from time to time. It is in the often tedious, mundane, monotonous grind of consistent discipline that significant breakthroughs occur. And those breakthroughs, my friend, tend to be truly inspiring for you and the world around you.

Running with Don

I had a humbling experience recently. I was in Virginia Beach visiting my brother Don, and he decided to join me for a run. I was scheduled for seven miles that day, and we went to a nearby park to "GIT R DUN." For the last year or so, I had been exercising consistently, including doing quite a bit of running. My brother had not. In fact, I'm guessing I had exercised at least six times as much as he had over the previous year, not to mention I'm two years younger. How do you think our run went?

It was no contest. He dusted me! I did my best to keep up for the first two or three miles while he placated me by staying close to my (exhausted) pace. Eventually I said, "Just go." I think he read a book, took a nap, and returned a few calls before I joined him at the end of the trail.

My brother is what you might call a "runner." I am not. Don ran track and cross country in high school and continued running as a young man in the Navy and into adulthood. I was a wrestler. Both of us have run a marathon. I trained consistently for over four months and barely broke five hours (4:52 to be precise). Don did not train. His time? (Wait for it...) 3 hours, 42 minutes. There is a high probability Don will always be a stronger runner than I am, and it never really bothered me... until that day. It just didn't seem right that I could work so hard for so long and still be so far from someone who, by comparison, apparently put in very little effort at all.

> "If you compare yourself to others, you may become vain and bitter; for always there will be greater and lesser persons than yourself."
> –Max Ehrmann

This is one of the potential traps we can fall into when we compare ourselves to others. We may become frustrated with what feels like lack of progress when we observe other people (particularly those close to us) functioning at a higher level. If we allow it to, this frustration may lead to abandoning a worthwhile journey prematurely or never taking the first step. It goes something like this, "I'll never be as (fast, strong, charismatic, talented, effective, successful, blah, blah, blah) as that person, so why bother?" When you find yourself thinking that way, consider the following:

- Look at the big picture. Is this process worthwhile for you as a person? Running and exercise is a powerful, healthy way for me to release stress, challenge myself, and be a better man. Whether or not I can keep up with my brother, you, or anybody else is irrelevant.

- Change your focus. Our greatest battles are won not over circumstances or other people but over ourselves. Are you being the best "you" that you can be?

The Ripple Effect

- Change the way you talk to yourself. Lose the "I'll nevers, I can'ts, I'm nots, and I won'ts." Affirm to yourself, "I am in the ring; I am growing; I am making progress."

- Learn. I asked Don how I could improve my pace, and he gave me a specific strategy which I implemented the following week.

- Allow yourself to be motivated. When I run with my brother, I have a choice: I can be depressed or inspired. Which do you think is healthier?

"The art of being yourself at
your best is the art of
unfolding your personality
into the person you want to be.
Be gentle with yourself, learn
to love yourself, to forgive
yourself, for only as we have
the right attitude toward
ourselves can we have the right
attitude toward others."
—Wilfred Peterson

How do you relate when comparing yourself
to others? Strive to be grateful for the people
who are put in your path. They are your
teachers, your students, your leaders, your
followers, your counselors, your advisors,
your lessons waiting to be learned.

Is it Time to Let Go?

> "In every block of marble I
> see a statue as plain as though
> it stood before me, shaped and
> perfect in attitude and action.
> I have only to hew away the
> rough walls that imprison the
> lovely apparition to reveal it
> to the other eyes as mine see
> it."
>
> –Michelangelo

The majority of the books, teachers, and courses I have learned from seem to focus on what we need to DO to improve ourselves. What strategies, actions, characteristics, or skills do we need to adopt? How can we grow, stretch, go for it, reach, make it happen? What's missing that we need to add to our lives?

The message appears to be that if I simply learn, grow, and push hard enough and long enough, and I become smart enough, I'll get there. Perhaps that's just how I tend to see the world: give up nothing, take on everything, more is better, anything is possible. Far less attention seems to be given to letting go of what's not working. What do we need to unlearn, eliminate, release?

If Michelangelo were chipping away at you, what would he get rid of? The intricate details of The David simply could not be introduced without first eliminating the large excesses which did not work. The same goes for fine tuning the masterpiece of your life. There may be one major thing, the "big block." You probably know what it is. Your big block prevents you from getting maximum benefit from your personal development efforts, no matter how hard, long, or innovative they may be. Eliminating your big block expands your current potential exponentially and brings new possibilities you may have never imagined.

Do you have a big block? It may include, but is not limited to:

- The past
- Unhealthy relationship(s)
- Alcohol
- Drugs
- Food
- Sex
- Work
- Gambling
- Anger
- Resentment
- Pride
- Fear
- Insecurity
- Cynicism

What are you holding on to? Is it time to let go?

The Naysayer

I remember several years ago calling on a prospect in California. When I introduced myself over the phone, he asked, "Are you the speaker who sings and plays the banjo?" I thought, *my reputation preceded me; how cool is that?* I smiled and said, "Yes, that's me!" He said, "Uh, yeah, I saw you last year; I don't think so" and hung up. It felt like I got punched in the stomach.

The Naysayer is everywhere, just waiting to say "NAY!" to your hopes, your dreams, and your future. When other people disapprove of our best efforts, we may feel deflated at best and at times downright debilitated.

Still harder for me to ignore is my internal Naysayer. He sounds a bit like Simon Cowell without the English accent.

On the boulevard of broken dreams there are countless unrealized talents and goals crushed by the Naysayer. Don't let that happen to you. Here are some thoughts on dealing with the Naysayers in your life or in your head.

- Don't take it personally. Easier said than done, right? But in many cases it's truly not personal. Hey—it's a banjo (or a new business, or a book you're writing, or a move to the country, or whatever). Not everybody gets it, so what? It doesn't take everybody to realize your dreams.
- Get used to it. Develop a thick skin. There will likely be many more naysayers along your journey.
- Get and stay around people who believe in you and lift you up. Tell those people how much you appreciate them.
- Don't try to please everyone; you never will, particularly the Naysayer.
- When you find yourself listening to your internal Naysayer, pick a different voice inside your head— one that appreciates you and believes in you. It's in there somewhere.

"There are many voices in my head. The key is choosing which one to listen to."
                                           –Doug Grady

Finally, appreciate the Naysayer, no matter how unwarranted, uninvited, inaccurate, or negative the feedback may appear to be. The Naysayer is a very real reminder that realizing our potential and achieving our goals isn't always easy. At times we may need to be humbled. At times we may needto be challenged. We may need a fire lit under us to grow, to stretch, and to get better. Let that be your response to the Naysayer.

Motivational Music

> "Music in the soul can be
> heard in the universe."
> —Lao Tzu

For as long as I can remember, music has been an important, powerful part of my life. Mom's angelic voice graced the choir every Sunday, and Dad sang and played piano and guitar. My brother, sister, and I took piano classes starting at age five and participated in the band and the choir. Roughly 10 years ago, I began singing and performing music during my speaking engagements. Getting together with friends for a little "pickin and grinnin" is one of my favorite things in life.

> "The power of music to
> integrate and cure... is the
> profoundest nonchemical
> medication."
> —Oliver Sacks

Did you ever make a mixed tape as a kid? Do you remember how some of the songs got on there? If your life were a movie, what would be on the soundtrack? The power of music is as close as your computer or mp3 player. Consider setting up a playlist titled "Motivational Music." Consciously choose songs that inspire you and move you to your core. List some of your favorite lyrics in your journal along with the musical artist. Why do they mean so much to you?

The X Factor

> *x fac•tor* (noun):
> 1. A variable in a situation that could have the most significant impact on the outcome.
> 2. A special talent or quality.
> –Dictionary.com

The X Factor, American Idol, The Voice, America's Got Talent—I watch them all from time to time. (Dancing with the Stars - not so much.) In addition to the absurd, ridiculous, and obscure auditions, there are those rare moments that keep me coming back.

Skyelor, a 16 year old from Mississippi, was on his first audition ever. It just happened to be in front of four of the most powerful people in music today, a 4,000 person crowd, and a TV audience of millions. Roughly 15 seconds into his song, the background music malfunctioned and stopped abruptly. Without missing a beat, Skyelor continued his audition. His spontaneous a cappella country crooning earned him a standing ovation and four yeses from the judges.

> "I came too far to stop."
> –Skyelor

Josh, a 30-something year old "burrito slinger" from Columbus, Ohio brought the house down with a spine tingling version of Etta James' "At Last My Love has Come Along." Simon remarked that after all his years in the business he never expected to be surprised, but Josh,

> "You blew me away."
> –Simon Cowell

I concur. He was phenomenal.

What is it about those unexpected moments from raw talent that move us so? Perhaps I should speak for myself. I had chills. It is that x-traordinary, x-ceptional, in-x-plicable X factor that I just can't get enough of.

My first acting coach, Martha Burgess, often referred to the best artists, actors, and performers as having the ability to "get people to feel." That is one of the reasons they are among the highest paid people on the planet.

How do you get to Carnegie Hall? Practice, practice, practice.

Here are some suggestions for developing your X Factor:

- **Practice.** Whether you are a salesman, a singer, or a senator, work hard to be the best you can be in your field of endeavor. Enroll in classes, attend seminars, keep growing. Practice, drill, rehearse.
- **Develop performance energy.** Before any event of significance, turn yourself on. Seek out experiences which get and keep you in a peak state.
- **Hire a coach.**

- **Put yourself on the line.** Whether your audience is a corporate decision maker, a family, or a large group consider seeking out experiences which frighten you just a bit. The energy from a prepared performance in a situation slightly out of your comfort zone is often a recipe for breakthrough results.
- **Connect.** Be present. Breathe. Listen, look, and feel the experience you are in.
- **Be inspired.** Allow yourself to be moved, even when sitting on the couch watching a show like The X Factor.

Getting Unstuck

> "Poker is a fascinating,
> wonderful, intricate adventure
> on the high seas of human
> nature."
> —David A. Daniel

I started playing poker in California in 2004. Some friends of mine started a poker league where I played consistently and learned the game. Eventually, I played tournaments and cash games on a regular basis, sometimes at fairly high stakes.

Poker is a game of decisions. In a perfect world, good decisions would always lead to winning and bad decisions would always lead to losing. In reality, because of the element of chance in poker, bad decisions can be rewarded and good decisions can cost you severely. It is not uncommon to see a very good player lose significant amounts of money in the short run.

Here are a couple of poker terms new players tend to learn very quickly:

stuck (adjective):
Losing, usually in a
particularly frustrating way,
or for a lot of money.
      –playwinningpoker.com

on tilt (adjective):
Upset or frustrated to an
extent that causes poor
decision making during game
play.
            –pokerzone.com

Whether or not you play poker, I am
guessing you have been stuck at one time or
another. Being stuck can take the form of a
financial setback, a sales slump, a
relationship that is not working, or a habit
you need to let go of. Getting stuck can be
the result of bad decisions, bad luck, or a
combination of the two.

      I guess if luck weren't
      involved I'd win every time."
                  –Phil Hellmuth

Here lies one of the major challenges in poker and in life. Losing, particularly while making good decisions, can lead a person to make bad decisions (go *on tilt*). This often compounds the problem, increasing losses exponentially. It goes something like this:

> decisions (good *or* bad) → bad outcome (stuck) → tilt → bad decisions → worse outcome (more stuck)

In poker, as in life…

- Bad decisions are often punished.
- Good decisions are not always rewarded and can lead to significant losses in the short run.
- Bad decisions + bad luck = stuck.
- Good decisions + bad luck = stuck.
- Being stuck can lead to more bad decisions.

Here are some thoughts on getting unstuck and staying off tilt.

"The deadly sin is to mistake
bad play for bad luck."
                    –Ian Fleming

1. Accurate analysis of your strategy is
   the first step to getting unstuck.
   Evaluate yourself. Seek the counsel
   of people you respect to help you
   with your analysis. Are you stuck
   because of:

   a. Bad luck?

   b. Bad decisions/strategy?

   c. Combination of both?

2. Take yourself out of the picture. One of the best pieces of advice I ever heard in poker was to play as if you had the best player you knew looking over your shoulder helping you. When it comes to the critical decisions in your business and in your life, this strategy is available to you at any time.

3. When it comes to bad luck, have a short term memory. Focus on the decision, not the outcome.

4. With regard to decisions, think long term. In poker, as in life, if you continue to make good decisions for long enough, you will win.

The Self-help Section

According to Marketdata Enterprises, a
Tampa-based research firm, Americans
spend more than $11 billion each year on
self-improvement products and services.
The self-help industry is expected to grow
6.2 percent annually over the next three
years.

> *If the self-help section worked
> it would be getting smaller,
> not larger.*
> —Self-help Conundrum

I remember attending a seminar in the mid
90s in which the speaker opened with the
above point. I had been in the self-help
industry for only a few short years at the
time. Now more than ever I can appreciate
both the humor and the truth in the
statement. My own internal need for growth
has often surfaced in various external
remedies and fixes which never quite get
there. My search for answers has led to more
questions. How much is within us and how
much do we need to discover? Is it more

important to learn or "unlearn"? When do I push and when do I let go? How can I best help others? *What is the difference that makes the difference?*

Recently, I made a trip to my local bookstore to check out some of the titles. Here are a few highlights...

Self-help book titles:

How to Make Anyone Fall in Love with You

The Secret Power of Middle Children

Put Your Big Girl Panties On

This is Why You're Fat

The Owner's Manual for the Brain (1005 pages)

The Procrastination Workbook

Change or Die

14000 Things to be Happy About

8789 Words of Wisdom

365 Ways to Boost Your Brain Power

287 Secrets of Reinventing Your Life

The 10 Women You'll be Before You're 35

5 Steps to a Quantum Life

The 4 Hour Work Week

The 30 Second Solution

The Ripple Effect (this is a really good one)

And finally...

The Only Book on Success You'll Ever Need, Volumes 1, 2, 3, 4, and 5 (OK, that one I made up)

Can a book really change your life? Or a seminar? Or hiring a coach? What does it take? *What is the difference that makes the difference?* What do **you** think?

Ironmen in Ecuador

> "As iron sharpens iron, so one
> man sharpens another."
> –Proverbs 27:17

Ironmen meet at Peachtree Presbyterian Church in Atlanta every Tuesday morning from 7-8am to teach and discuss ideas and strategies on being better men. From June 11-18, 2010, twelve of us went to Ecuador to build nine homes in the slums of Guayaquil in conjunction with Hogar de Cristo. That was the fourth year for the trip; it was my first.

Day 1: We arrived in Guayaquil, Ecuador late Friday night after a five plus hour flight. Half of us had been bumped up to first class, so we weren't exactly roughing it. I contemplated the irony of our good fortune contrasted with our mission to help the poorest of the poor. Our accommodations: a serene Catholic retreat center called Schoenstatt Casa de Retiro. We settled in for a big day ahead of us.

Day 2: Saturday morning, after grabbing supplies at the local hardware store, all 12 of us went to the first building site. I have never seen poverty like this first hand. It gave me new understanding of the term "dirt poor." With the help of our "maestros," Ivan and Gato, we completed the building of our first Hogar de Cristo home by 4:30pm. What impressed me most the first day were the smiles and laughter of the children in the neighborhood. We seemed to be the local entertainment for the day. We were a bit overmanned at times, and I was able to break off and visit with some of the local children.

While language was a bit of a barrier (mi Espanola no es muy bueno), we found some common ground in the King of Pop. Yes, Michael Jackson has fans in the slums of Ecuador. The MJ dance-off was one of the many highlights of the day. Seeing a mother and her five children smiling on the steps of their newly built home topped them all.

Day 3: On our second day of building, we broke off into two teams. Chuck Roberts lead our team and Gato was our chosen maestro. We traveled to a very remote area in the outskirts of Guayaquil to build for an elderly woman—the sole caretaker of a

young boy with Down's syndrome. She had taken him in when nobody else wanted him. To the side of the building area there was a mattress, a small grill, and a bag of clothing. I was informed later that those items were 100% of the possessions of that woman and child. By 3:30pm, they were smiling on the steps of their new home.

Day 4: We built homes four and five today. That property seemed a bit more "upscale" comparatively—it was fenced off, across from a school, and had a bunch of chickens and a couple of dogs running around. We had a bit of a competition going with the other team to see who could complete the build faster. (We lost that one.). We were blessed with clouds that sheltered us from the hot, Ecuadorian sun and all in all it was a pleasant day of work and mixing with locals. By 3pm a mother and her five children were moving in.

Day 5: We toured the Hogar de Cristo facilities. Hogar de Cristo's mission is to help the "poorest of the poor,"

mostly women and children, many of whom suffer from severe hunger, malnutrition, and abuse. In addition to building on average 50 houses per day for the homeless, HDC is producing and distributing soy milk to children in schools. Last year it resulted in a 20% reduction in the number of children with severe anemia. Luis Tavara, director of HDC, told us the reason he enjoyed working with the Ironmen group every year was because of our smiles. He said our smiles conveyed hope and possibility to the people we met in the slums of Ecuador. I thought to myself how great it was seeing the families we met smile, and I made a personal commitment to smile more.

Day 6: We built homes six and seven—another "typical" situation: We built for a single mother with five children from several different fathers, none of whom were around. I really enjoyed the kids, especially Esteban. He was a little firecracker—laughing, running around, constantly

babbling (although I have no idea what he was talking about) and just having a great time. Apparently, no one had told him he was poor, and he must've forgotten that he was hungry. He was just a kid being a kid—a happy kid. Early in the trip, Chuck had asked us to be aware of where we saw God. I saw Him in the children. I saw Him in their enthusiasm. I saw Him in their smiles. I was reminded of that old song,

"Jesus loves the little children, all the children of the world. Red or yellow, black or white, they're all precious in his sight. Jesus loves the little children of the world."

Day 7: Each of the two teams completed their final builds today (Numbers eight and nine). I was present to a bit of sadness and a lot of gratitude. More than one out of ten people in Ecuador are homeless. Guayaquil has the third highest percentage of homeless people of any major city in the world. They are born into it, and the vast majority will be in it the rest of their lives. We put nine of those homeless families into homes, and I grateful to have been a part of it. I am grateful for the men who made the trip happen. I am grateful for my family and friends who supported me in participating. I am grateful for the many blessings in my life. I am grateful to have served. I am grateful for the many smiles of the men, women, and children we met along the way.

Day 8: We said "Hasta la vista" to Guayaquil, Ecuador. I had a hard time coming up with the proper adjective to describe that experience. It had been humbling, enlightening, beautiful, exhausting, extraordinary, saddening, uplifting... Eight days in Guayaquil, nine houses built, nine families with homes, 12 men forever changed. I, for one, will be smiling more often.

Gratitude

In October 2011, I went on my second trip to Wellington, AL. My church organized the trip to help out those whose lives have been devastated by the storms that ravaged the southeast earlier that year. It is unlikely it would have been on my radar before I participated in my first mission trip. Today I reflected on the ripple effect from Ironmen in Ecuador.

> "Gratitude can turn a meal
> into a feast."
> –Melody Beattie

In June of 2010, I went to Ecuador for eight days with 11 other men from my church. We built nine homes in the slums of Guayaquil. One of the things that impressed me most about the homeless families that we met was the sheer joy they exuded—especially the children. They were happy, truly happy— just running around laughing and kicking a half-deflated soccer ball. I had more money in my pocket than most of those families would see in months. How could they be so happy with so little? How could I be so frustrated and stressed with so much? When things are tough for me, I may wonder where my next speaking engagement is coming from. On a good day, they may wonder where their next meal is coming from.

Boli Alfaro was one of our leaders. He also happens to be the great grandson of Eloy Alfaro, the President of Ecuador from 1895 to 1901 and 1906 to 1911. He posed a couple of questions before giving thanks for our evening meal. Why were we born with so many advantages? Why were they born into such severe poverty with so little chance of ever getting out?

> "Why them and not me?"
> –Boli Alfaro

Why them and not me? How did I get so lucky? It certainly was through no power of my own. Everything I am or ever hope to be was given to me. The country I live in, the family I was born into, the education I received, my strengths, talents, and potential... these are God-given gifts. Of course I have the power to choose, but this too is a gift. The sheer magnitude of choices I have simply does not exist for the people we served in Ecuador.

We have been given talents, and we complain about our faults. We make progress, and we remain cynical. We have breakthroughs, and we continue to be bitter. OK, maybe it's just me.

Another man shared with me his initial reluctance to participate in that mission trip. His reasoning was that with so many problems in our own country, why go to another to serve? I could relate to his logic. Then I looked at my life. I never did much of anything to serve in my own back yard. It took a mission trip in another country for me to become grateful for what I have at home. It took going to Ecuador to get me to Wellington, AL.

Rescued

This year, my church organized several trips to Wellington, AL to help those whose lives were devastated by the storms that ravaged the southeast. I went on two of those trips, most recently Saturday, October 15, 2011.

Wellington, AL sits in tornado alley where storms are a common occurrence. April 27, 2011 was many things to many people in Wellington. "Common" is not one of them. Their stories are incredible, riveting, and almost unbelievable.

Jerry has lived there for most of his life with his children and grandchildren living a stone's throw away. They rarely heeded his call through the years to take shelter at his place during the frequent tornado warnings. On that day, however, they came. Just as the last two arrived, the tornado hit. All 13 of them were protected in Jerry's basement as their homes were completely destroyed. Jerry's was the only home with a basement.

Jerry introduced us to Joey. He told us his story.

"Hold on baby!" Joey yelled as he and his wife were sucked into the air by the force of the tornado. He kept a firm grip on one of her arms while the rest of her was flapping in the wind. When the storm had passed, their home, car, and most of their possessions had been blown out of sight. They found themselves on the ground among the scattered debris that remained, wrapped in each other's arms, unharmed.

Jerry told us of another incident not too far away. A large tree had fallen during the storm pushing a mother and her child into the earth below. A punctured lung left her unable to make a sound, while her child was silenced from shock. The glancing eyes of their injured dog told rescuers where to look, saving them both. The family dog died as they were both pulled to safety.

These are three of the amazing stories from April 27, 2011 in Wellington, AL. I felt honored to hear them and compelled to share them. Jerry, Joey, and many others are still picking up the pieces and rebuilding their homes, their community, and their lives. May the good Lord continue to bless the community of Wellington.

Vision Repaired

I thought I was just tired. I was reading a book with fine print and found myself pushing it further away to make out the words. My vision was better than 20/20—it had to be a mistake. I delayed the inevitable for over two-and-a-half years. Finally, I faced the facts and bought my first pair of reading glasses.

> "It is a terrible thing to see
> and have no vision."
> –Helen Keller

What are the factors causing us to resist simple shifts that can significantly improve the quality of our lives? Here are some that have popped up for me:

- Comfort zone. Sometimes I like to hold on to my old, familiar way of looking at things—even if it doesn't work so well anymore.
- Blind spots. I got so used to reading with obscured vision, I almost didn't notice it.

- Self comparison. While it is true that I am continuing to improve in various areas of my life, apparently eyesight is not one of them. Comparing myself to how I used to be can be a recipe for frustration.
- Denial. I simply did not want to accept my limitations.
- Pride/ego/vanity. Glasses, when I got right down to it, represented weakness in my mind. I didn't want to rely on something outside myself to get results I was used to getting on my own.

I just happened to be with a trusted friend who reminded me how absurd my stubbornness was. Without that gentle prodding, it is likely I would still be vision impaired. As I write these words (glasses on), I am wondering what took me so long.

"Where there is no vision, the people perish."
—Proverbs 29:18

Tools, resources, and strategies are all around us. They come in the form of books, trainings, people... and glasses. What are you doing today to improve your vision?

The Four Levels of Integrity

Here's my simple definition of integrity:

Integrity: The act of doing what you said you would do when you said you would do it.

It is a yes or no scenario. You either did or you didn't. Missing a deadline, skipping a scheduled workout, or eating something you said you wouldn't eat are all examples of integrity lacking. When it comes to developing a new habit, eliminating a bad habit, or developing a daily discipline, keeping your word isn't always easy.

In striving to live a life of integrity, I have noticed the *way* in which I do so is not always the same. In evaluating patterns in my life and the lives of others, I have distinguished four distinct ways in which integrity occurs. I call these the four levels of integrity.

Level One Integrity – The Carrot and the Stick

Level One Integrity is externally motivated and primarily driven by the desire to avoid external pain (the stick) and to gain external pleasure (the carrot).

> "The secret of success is learning how to use pain and pleasure instead of having pain and pleasure use you."
> –Tony Robbins

In my second year in as an agent in the insurance business, I set two records within a three month period. One of the disciplines I engaged in was making a minimum of 25 prospecting calls each business day for 11 weeks. My carrot: the coveted President's ring. My stick: I was required to work Sundays if I did not reach my weekly sales goals. Consciously setting up a structure which rewards desired behavior and discourages unwanted behavior is a critical success skill.

Examples of (external) pain:

- April 15th
- Obeying the speed limit in an area known to have law enforcement
- Depriving yourself of something fun (TV, internet, recreation) until you have fulfilled your commitment(s). Brian Tracy calls this "dinner before dessert."

Examples of (external) pleasure:

- Showing up on time or early to impress your boss
- Pushing to qualify for a company trip, President's club, or other incentive
- Buying a new dress if you reach your intended weight

The power of the carrot and the stick is available at any time. You can create personal incentives for sticking to your daily commitments and reaching milestones. You can impose sanctions for not honoring your word or not reaching a goal.

The major drawbacks of relying too heavily on Level One Integrity fall generally into two categories:

1. Getting hit with the stick may at times feel better than honoring your commitment.
2. You may decide your carrot is not worth the effort and break your commitment.

Choose your carrot and stick wisely, as well as the structure in which it is enforced. Be careful not to put too much stock in the carrot or the stick. It is your personal integrity, not external forces, which must reign supreme.

Level Two Integrity: Do it Anyway

> "Becoming aware of where
> you get stopped is the starting
> point of becoming
> unstoppable."
>
> –Doug Grady

One of the most valuable aspects of taking on a new habit or daily discipline is becoming aware of your tendencies; realizing where and how you tend to get stopped. Understanding and consciously evaluating your personal tendencies can be a major step in becoming unstoppable. Let me share with you one of mine.

I tend to have an "all or nothing" mentality. If I can't do something full on, why bother? In March of 2010, I sustained a hip injury while training for a half marathon. I allowed the injury to become an excuse for not exercising. The lack of exercise led to several months of a sedentary lifestyle and exacerbated a downward spiral in other areas of my life. Now think about it; Are there ways to exercise even if you have a hip injury? Of course there are. Recognizing that tendency enabled me to adopt a new belief:

When it comes to exercise and other daily commitments, something is better than nothing.

Level Two Integrity succeeds where Level One fails. While Level One is primarily driven by the desire to gain external pleasure and avoid external pain, Level Two is internally driven. If you are taking on creating a new habit, breaking a bad habit, or developing a daily discipline, you will inevitably experience times when you simply don't want to honor your word. On days like that, you simply find a way to DO IT ANYWAY. You do it because you said you would. Whether you want to or not or feel like it or not; whether you think it will do any good or not. All those questions are really irrelevant. The only question is:

Are you going to honor your word? Are you going to do what you said you would do?

During a 60-day commitment to write 20 minutes a day, there were times I literally sat at the computer when I was running late for a dinner engagement, typing while the seconds ticked away toward approaching 20 minutes. I typed, looked at the clock, typed, looked at the clock…

During a 30-day commitment to make 20 prospecting calls per day, there were days when I simply went through the motions of dialing just to check it off the list. Inevitably, those were days when I reached someone previously unreachable and booked an elusive meeting. I also had a couple of personal bests in the gym on days I did not feel like exercising.

> "I hate working out. I do it because this is my job. I hate working out so much that when I get in the ring I take it out on my opponent."
> –Quinton 'Rampage' Jackson

Never underestimate the power of getting it done when you don't feel like it. It is here in the often tedious, mundane, monotonous act of completion that significant momentum is gained. There may be days when you simply put in the time—you complete the tired, lethargic, irritating work. Feel the frustration, feel the pain, hear the excuse, and do it anyway. The win here is that YOU DID IT! You fulfilled your commitment. No one said it had to be pretty or pleasant.

There is HUGE power in completion versus the lack thereof. Notice and track how you feel after you did it anyway—when you did not feel like it, did not want to, and considered not doing it at all. Those moments are the precursors to breakthroughs.

It is extremely difficult to maintain Level Two Integrity over an extended period of time. There is a constant struggle between feelings ("I don't feel like it.") and commitment ("I'll do it anyway."). Relying purely on will power can be exhausting and unhealthy in the long run. That is where Level Three Integrity comes in.

Level Three Integrity: I like Green Eggs

Take a moment right now to think of a few foods you particularly disliked when you were younger but now enjoy as an adult. For me, there were Brussels sprouts, broccoli, spinach, and eggplant. As a child, I was required to eat those foods because they were "good for me." I certainly would not have eaten them if I had not been made to. I now choose to eat them, and I enjoy them (except eggplant – I still dislike eggplant). As far as I know, Brussels sprouts have not changed much in the last 30 years; what changed was my perspective.

This is the essence of moving from Level Two to Level Three Integrity. Here the superficial forces of Level One are much less of a factor (if at all). The "because I said I would" drive of Level Two (an avoidance mechanism) does not occur to you. Your daily commitments become an act of self-expression, completely consistent with who you are becoming. They become positive, powerful, pleasant choices. Your workouts, calls, reading, meditation, writing, or other activities are now your lifestyle. Your commitments may not have changed, but your perspective has. It is an extraordinarily empowering moment when "have to" becomes "want to" and "get to."

> "I like green eggs and ham! I
> like them, Sam-I-am!"
> –Dr. Seuss

While both Level Two and Level Three Integrity are driven internally, that is where the similarity ends. Here's a breakdown:

L2	L3
Internal	Internal
Avoidance driven	Moving toward
Will power	Want power
Destination	Journey
GIT-R-DUN	Enjoy the process
Means to an end	Self-expression
Have to	Get to/want to
Chore	Choice

Living in Level Three is truly living at a higher level. It is there we often feel a sense of passion, purpose, and progress. From a purely practical standpoint, it is much easier to maintain your commitments when they are enjoyable rather than something you do purely out of duty or obligation. Furthermore, while there are exceptions, the quality of output generated will tend to be superior to that of Level One or Level Two.

There is, however, another level…

Level Four Integrity: Throw Your Hat in the Ring

> In the early 19th century when boxing was quite popular, one who wished to challenge a boxer would throw his hat into the ring. That was probably necessitated by the crowds and noise at such events; you'd be missed if you simply tried to shout out a challenge or push your way through the crowd and into the ring. Theodore "Teddy" Roosevelt used it in 1912: "My hat's in the ring", he said, meaning that he had entered the presidential race.
>
> –www.phrases.org.uk

While I was talking with my friend Jerry, she asked me,

"What's your next accomplishment you are going after?"

–Jerry Bishop

I had recently completed my first Tough Mudder, a series of breakthrough speaking engagements, and written *The (unofficial) Tough Mudder Song*. But I had not thrown my hat into another ring for something new, specific, and time lined. I had been thinking about writing a song for my mother. Thinking about it for almost three years— first for her 70th birthday, then on subsequent Mother's Days and birthdays, and then on my parents' 50th wedding anniversary

> *throw your hat in the ring*
> (verb):
> the act of making a definite, time-bounded, external declaration of what you intend to take on or accomplish.
>
> –Doug Grady

Here is my response to Jerry:

> "I am taking on writing and recording a song for my mother and posting it on her Facebook page on Sunday."

Mother's Day was less than three days away. I literally created and completed more in those three days than I had the previous three years combined. It seemed almost effortless. The completed video of *Ode to my Mother* was on her Facebook page on Mother's Day, and she loved it.

Had I not thrown my hat in the ring, it is likely that song would have still been rolling around in my head next Mother's Day. That is the power of Level Four Integrity. It combines the best of Level Three with powerful external motivation. When you have an empowering future, it gives meaning, purpose, passion, and intensity to your daily commitments NOW.

Do you want to:

- Play the guitar? Sing? Do stand-up comedy? Book an open mic night.

- Lose weight? Register for a run, hire a trainer, buy the clothes you will fit into.

- Take a vacation? Call the hotel and give them a non-refundable deposit for a specific date.

- Start a business? Get the business card printed. File for a business license.

- Increase your sales? Register for a sales seminar, hire a coach, book a celebration date now for 3 months out.

- Write a book? Design the cover and look at it daily.

I leave you with the question Jerry asked me: "What's your next accomplishment you are going after?" And a challenge...

Throw your hat in the ring!

Note: Be aware of what level of integrity you are operating in. I recommend you track your level daily. Avoid self-judgment and don't attempt to force yourself into a higher level. Simply notice and track. Keep in mind you will likely ebb and flow back and forth between levels. Just when you think you have "arrived" at Level Three or Level Four, the next day you may be back at Level One. This is normal. Simply notice where you are and continue to honor your choice.

On the next page is a simple tracking tool I developed and used during a 30 day commitment to exercise. Feel free to use it, modify it, or create your own.

Day	Commitment	Actual	Y/N	Level	Ripples
1	exercise 30 min	33 min jog	Y	2	got it done!!
2	exercise 30 min	42 min weights	Y	1	1st time in 3 months
3	exercise 30 min	75 min yoga	Y	3	felt great
4	exercise 30 min	Spin 60 min	Y	4	registered-Mudder
5					

Choice

One simple choice can change the course of your life.

You can choose right now to reconnect with your higher purpose. You can take the first step toward an unrealized passion or let go of an unhealthy habit. You can throw your hat in the ring. You can choose a daily, weekly, or monthly commitment. You can choose to do nothing at all. Each choice will have ripples.

Don't worry about making the perfect choice. Perfectionism nourishes procrastination and can keep you stuck. Choose something. Choose simply. Choose powerfully. Choose now.

> "Character is the ability to carry out a good resolution long after the excitement of the moment has passed."
> –Cavett Robert

Honoring your choice will not always be easy. Don't let your ripple die the death of most New Year's resolutions.
Breakthroughs happen in the daily grind of consistently doing what you said you would do. The road ahead will undoubtedly contain many twists and turns; unexpected pain and exciting breakthroughs; setbacks and victories.

> "I took the road less traveled,
> now I have no idea where in
> the world I am."
>
> –Anonymous

Become acutely aware of what is showing up in your life. This is source of the power of the ripple effect. Record in your journal:

- What level of integrity did you operate in today?

- What ripples[2] are surfacing?

- How do you feel?

Finally, share with others you know what you are doing and your ripples. This is in essence how this book came to be.

Welcome to *The Ripple Effect*.

---

[2] "Ripples" are defined as the breakthroughs, experiences, realizations, people, things, additional commitments, and other results showing up in your life since you made your choice.

About the Author

Doug Grady has been studying and teaching the pathways to personal potential for over 20 years. Exciting, entertaining and enlightening are words invariably used to describe his unique seminars and workshops. Doug is an entrepreneur, musician, and author. He is President of High Achievers, and is owner or co-owner of three additional companies. His companies, writings, trainings, and music are designed with one purpose: to help people reach their God-given potential.

Doug gives a significant portion of his time and money to service, including local and global mission trips. He is a table leader at Peachtree Ironmen, dedicated to encouraging and equipping men to become a positive impact for Jesus at home, at work, and in the community. Doug is an active member of Peachtree Presbyterian Church in Atlanta, GA.

High Achievers is a global community of people embracing a lifestyle of achievement. Our networks, events, trainings, challenges, and memberships put you on the path to reach your highest potential.

We believe in the power of mentors, coaches, networks, and training.

We believe in professional growth through personal growth.

We believe in the power of the human spirit.

Connect with Doug

http://www.douggrady.com
http://www.Facebook.com/douggradytraining
http://twitter.com/douggrady
http://www.linkedin.com/in/douggrady
http://www.youtube.com/user/douggvideo
http://www.highachieversnetwork.com/blog

Connect with High Achievers

http://www.highachievers.com
http://www.Facebook.com/HighAchieversNetwork
http://twitter.com/achievernetwork
http://highachieversnetwork.com/membership
http://www.blogtalkradio.com/highachiever

1) Linked In
* Photo
* NAME
* what I do exactly
* where I am
* name + webpage

The Ripple Effect